Lord, Can We Talk This Over?

Lord, Can We Talk This Over?

by
Joy P. Gage

MOODY PRESS
CHICAGO

© 1980 by
THE MOODY BIBLE INSTITUTE
OF CHICAGO

Gage, Joy P.
Lord, can we talk this over?

1. Moses. 2. Faith—Biblical teaching. 3. Bible. O.T. Exodus—Study. 4.
Bible. N.T. Hebrews XI, 23-29—Study. I. Title.
BS580.M6G257   222'.10924   80-16014
ISBN 0-8024-4011-8

Printed in the United States of America

For Ken
who has opened to me
the Word of God

CONTENTS

Introduction   9
1. No Turning Back   15
2. Please Send Somebody Else!   23
3. God, Why Did You Bring Me Here?   31
4. Look What Happened Tomorrow!   39
5. A Promise Is a Promise Is a Promise   47
6. If You're Not Going, Lord, Don't Send Me   55
7. Battle Fatigue, Complaints, and Critics 63
8. Miracles, Mercies, and Myopia   71
9. The Disobedient Are Dispensable   79
10. The Last Word   87

CONTENTS

Introduction

1. ...
2. ...

Introduction

Exodus 14; Hebrews 11:23-29

Faith as man defines it is not always faith as God decrees it. Too often man limits faith to the mustard seed variety that moves mountains. The tiny seed enshrouded in cold, clear plastic becomes a symbol of his belief in some mysterious force that is neither explainable nor attainable.

Yet a look at what God calls faith reveals that it is neither mysterious nor unreachable. Over a dozen individuals named in Hebrews 11 are said to have exercised faith on specific occasions. The people of Israel are said to have exercised faith corporately in passing through the Red Sea. That "Red Sea" variety of faith demonstrated a most rudimentary type of obedience, and nothing more. The record shows that at the time of Israel's crossing, the people were convinced they were going to die; they were terrified of Pharaoh's armies; and they were doubtful whether or not they should have left Egypt. Hemmed in on all sides, they crossed the sea because they found no other options. Few men would regard that as faith. But God did. Regardless of their mental state, the Israelites crossed the sea as God had directed, and in so doing they obeyed Him. That simple act of obedience was in God's sight an act of faith. In fact, obedience played a major role in many of the actions designated in Hebrews 11, the chapter known as faith's Hall of Fame.

Moses commands more space in that chapter than does any other individual except Abraham. Despite the fact that his name is practically synonymous with the Law, it is from Moses' life that we gain some of Scripture's most practical lessons on faith. The record of his life spans four Bible books and reveals a myriad of struggles that are not unlike those of the twentieth-century believer. His faith began with a definite commitment and climaxed with a direct confronta-

9

tion in which Moses moved not a mountain but the God who made the mountain. Between those two points he had to deal with failure, self-doubts, and discouragement. His obedience was sometimes reluctant, his steps often hesitant. Yet the day came when Moses moved God by reminding Him, "Lord, You promised, You promised, You promised!"

It would be terribly discouraging, as well as very deceptive, to look at that dramatic encounter as a separate incident. Our picture of Moses' faith is much more accurate if we begin with his first encounter, in which he adamantly declared, "Lord, I can't, I can't, I can't." His great lesson to us is that faith grows as we meet each obstacle openly and honestly.

The progress of his faith is vividly recorded in Moses' dialogues with the Lord. Although I have taught the life of Moses for many years, only recently have I discovered the importance of those dialogues. From the first word spoken at the burning bush to the last word uttered on Mount Pisgah, those conversations have proved to be a rich source of inspiration. From that discovery this book has grown.

It is not intended to be the last word on faith.

It is not intended to be the last word on Moses.

It is a simple account of some dialogues in which I found an intimate journal of one man's faith and how it grew.

Study Guide
IS FAITH SOMETHING YOU DO?
Scripture: Exodus 14, Hebrews 11

HOW WOULD YOU DESCRIBE FAITH? The statements below are descriptive rather than definitive. Each statement should be judged on the basis of whether it says something true about faith, not on whether it is a complete definition of faith. With that in mind, read the sentences carefully. Cross out all statements with which you disagree.

    A. Faith is something you feel.
    B. Faith is something you believe.
    C. Faith is something you do.
    D. Faith is making a commitment that affects your life.
    E. Faith is an unshakable confidence that God can do anything.
    F. Faith is doing what is right because you are not afraid.
    G. Faith is obedience to God when neither B, D, E, nor F̄ is true.

HOW DOES GOD DESCRIBE FAITH? Scripture Exercise

    To discover how God describes faith, read Hebrews 11. Notice the various actions that were said to have been done in faith. Also note any indication of attitudes present (belief, etc.). Complete the following exercise:

Verses 17-19. Who was the individual said to have exercised faith

in these verses? _____What did he do by faith?
_____ What does
verse 19 tell you about his attitude? _____
What specific thing did he believe? _____
_____
Verse 23. Who were the individuals who acted in faith in this verse?
_____ What did they do?
_____ What does the
verse tell you about their attitude? _____
_____
Verses 24-25. How would you describe the act of faith that is
recorded in these verses? _____
_____
Verse 29. To whom does the word "they" refer? _____
_____
What did they do by faith?_____
_____
Is there anything in this verse to indicate their attitude at the time of
the action? _____ Now read Exodus 14:8-22 and answer the
following questions. Describe briefly the scene prior to the crossing
of the sea by the Israelites. _____
_____
What was Israel's state of mind (v. 10)? _____
What did the people say (vv. 11-12)?_____
_____ In spite of their
attitude, what action did they take? _____
_____

SUMMARIZE: On the basis of this Scripture exercise we see that
items B through G of the first exercise may be said to be descriptive
of faith. To help complete the picture of faith as God sees it, match
the statements below by drawing a line to the individual who evidenced faith as described.

Abraham   A. Faith is doing what is right because you
                      are not afraid.

Moses' parents   B. Faith is making a commitment that af-
                      fects your life.

Moses

Israelites

C. Faith is an unshakable confidence that God can do anything.

D. Faith is doing what God says when none of the above is true.

IS FAITH SOMETHING YOU DO? Yes, when it is something done because God told you to do it. Think of this: "If simple obedience is so important to God that He calls it faith, how may I better give evidence of faith this week?"

1
No Turning Back
Exodus 1-2; Acts 7:21-29; Hebrews 11:24-25

In reconstructing the growth of Moses' faith, it is essential that we begin at a point in time some forty years before the first recorded dialogue. A decision made by Moses at that time was judged by God to be an act of faith. Hebrews 11:24-25 records his decision. He relinquished his standing as the son of Pharaoh's daughter in order to identify himself with Pharaoh's slaves.

The Israelites had been slaves for many generations when Moses was born into a family of Levi's tribe. The book of Exodus opens at a juncture in Hebrew history when the slaves were beginning to outnumber the Egyptians. Such proliferation posed some problems to Pharaoh. What if the slaves rebelled? What if they sided with some future warring enemy?

To insure their subjection, Pharaoh forced the slaves to work under harsh labor conditions. Brick and mortar became the keys to survival as they were compelled to produce the materials needed for Egypt's storage cities. Driven by cruel taskmasters, they constructed the thick-walled bins into which the grain of Egypt was poured for safekeeping. Where there had been comfortable servitude, now there was bitter bondage and no hope of relief. Still the Israelites multiplied. Pharaoh, determined to suppress them, devised a rather drastic method of population control. All male slave babies were to be killed at birth. Into such a time was Moses born.

The faith of Moses' parents prompted them to hide their infant son. Their fearless action led to the adoption of Moses into the household of Pharaoh. Into a carefully prepared basket they placed their baby. While an older sister, Miriam, watched from a distance, the basket was left to float on the Nile. When Pharaoh's daughter found him and claimed him for her own, Moses entered into a life-style that was radically different from that of his less fortunate Hebrew brethren. Growing up in the palace afforded him every educational advantage available in the very center of civilization. For forty years, he enjoyed all that the palace confines had to offer. While he became skilled in word and deed, his fellow Hebrews became bitter and resigned to their lot. While he learned his lessons under the care of a tutor, they baked adobes under the whip of an overseer. For them life consisted of long hours and hard labor. For him, there was luxury and security.

Then one day Moses, the slave who had become a prince, went for a walk in the brickyards. All the problems that he had escaped for four decades suddenly became his as he saw sweating slaves harassed and tormented by the Egyptians. Believing that God had sent him to deliver the slaves, he immediately began a one-man "Help the Hebrews" campaign. He was sure the slaves would understand that God had sent him. But they did not.

His crusade lasted exactly two days. On the first, Moses saw an Egyptian beating a slave. He intervened. In the fracas he killed the Egyptian and disposed of the body by hiding it in the sand. On the second day, to his dismay, he found two slaves quarreling. He stepped in and reprimanded the one at fault. It seemed a logical move. After all, why should people who were so oppressed fight among themselves? Was not unity an essential factor in any liberation attempt? Whatever his reasoning, his advice was not appreciated. "Who made you a judge over us?" the brawling Hebrew spit at Moses. How bitterly he must have flung the words into the face of his would-be deliverer.

One can easily surmise other questions implied here. "Who needs you—you with your Egyptian ways and prince's robes?"

"What have you been doing all these years while we've been slaving away for the great pharaoh?" They understood nothing except that their self-appointed judge was a despised Egyptian inside Hebrew skin. So ended the brief crusade.

In the brickyards nothing had changed. For Moses, nothing would ever be the same.

In the immediate failure it is easy to lose sight of the act of faith here recorded. It was the decision, not the attempted deliverance, that was important. Moses made a definite choice. He gave up one thing in favor of another. His involvement in the brickyard was no mere humanitarian impulse. Moses knew he had to forsake the comforts of the palace and take his place with the children of Israel. God's people. His people.

It was a turning point in Moses' life. Overnight his life-style was drastically changed. In fear for his life because the incident involving the Egyptian was known, Moses fled to Midian. There he traded his princely robes for shepherd's garb and spent the next four decades leading around a flock of sheep. There is absolutely no indication whatever that he regretted his decision. That fact presents an inescapable contrast between Moses and the people he ultimately delivered.

When the great exodus came, the slaves were halfheartedly looking for a better life. When it failed to materialize immediately, they vacillated. The farther from Egypt they were removed, the better Egypt looked. They forgot the bondage and romanticized the past. In their hearts they constantly turned back to Egypt. They blamed Moses for every discomfort. "Why didn't you leave us alone? We want to go back!" Humanly speaking, those were complaints by a people who had left nothing, registered against a leader who had left everything. Yet the leader never once retaliated with, "Why did I ever leave that palace?"

Recently a member of my husband's congregation came to him with one of those "Pastor, what shall I do?" situations. It seems that a couple whom he had been discipling was trying to find the best of two worlds. The pair had enthusiastically responded to a home Bible study program with him, but they continued their participation in many practices that were morally and legally questionable.

17

Needless to say, their spiritual progress was nil. My husband was quick to point out to that teacher that without a personal commitment there is nothing upon which to build.

Progress begins with a definite choice. When Moses refused to be called the son of Pharaoh's daughter and chose to suffer with his brethren, his decision was final. Whatever the future held, there was no turning back. We call that commitment. Some call it burning one's bridges.

God calls it faith.

Study Guide
WHY IS COMMITMENT IMPORTANT TO THE LIFE OF THE BELIEVER?

SCRIPTURE: Acts 7:17-29; Exodus 1:1—2:15; Hebrews 11:23-26

WHAT PROMPTED MOSES TO HELP THE ISRAELITES? Our lesson has focused on the period of Moses' life when he first attempted to help Israel. He was still living in the palace, and his "Help the Hebrews" campaign was short-lived. The statements below give some possible reasons for Moses' attempt to help the Israelites at that point. Cross out all those with which you disagree.

   A. Moses felt guilty about his life-style when he saw his own people in the brickyards.
   B. Moses was a humanitarian at heart and would have helped anyone in trouble.
   C. The Scriptures give no clue as to his motives.
   D. Moses was sure that God had called him to the task.

Now read Acts 7:22-25 and check that against your answer.

HOW SUCCESSFUL WAS MOSES? Scripture Exercise, Part 1

   How did his campaign change the lives of the Hebrews? (Exodus 1:7-16; 2:11-14). Notice the condition of the Hebrews, the actions of Moses, and the reactions of the Hebrews. Complete the following exercise.

Verses 1:8-10. The king of Egypt saw that the Israelites were (underline correct answer) (a) weak in number (b) growing in numbers (c) already more than the Egyptians. The king was (underline correct answer) (a) comfortable with the situation (b) apprehensive about the future. Two things the king feared are revealed in verse 10. He was afraid the Israelites would _____ Egypt's enemies and _____ against Egypt. He was afraid the end result of that would be that the Israelites would "get . . . up _____ of the _____."

Verses 11-12. What did the king of Egypt do to the Israelites? ___

_____

Did that accomplish the desired results? _____
Verses 15-16. What drastic measure did the king try next? _____

_____
_____

Verse 17. Why did the plan fail? _____

_____

Verse 22. Note that Pharaoh then repeated his order, this time involving more than the midwives. Whom did he charge with killing the sons? _____

Acts 7:23-25. How old was Moses when he went out to his brethren in the brickyards? _____

Exodus 2:11. What did Moses see? _____

_____

Describe the incident that followed. _____

_____

Verse 13. On the next day when Moses observed another fight, who were the principals involved? _____
How did Moses handle the situation? _____

_____

Verse 14. Was he successful as a peacemaker? _____
Verses 14-15. How did his attempt to help the Israelites end? ___

_____

Had Moses changed the living conditions of the Israelites at all?

_____

HOW DID MOSES' INVOLVEMENT WITH THE ISRAELITES CHANGE HIS OWN LIFE-STYLE? Scripture Exercise, Part 2
    Verses 2:10, 15. Where he had once lived in the p _ _ _ _ _, now

20

he fled to M _ _ _ _ _. Exodus 2:21; 3:1. Once he had been a prince, now he became a s _ _ _ _ _ _ _. Exodus 2:21-22. He was c _ _ _ _ _ _ to dwell with his father-in-law in Midian, but he called himself a s _ _ _ _ _ _ _ in a s _ _ _ _ _ _ l _ _ _.

From a human perspective, Moses' campaign to help the Israelites may be said to have been completely unsuccessful. Not only did he accomplish nothing for the Israelites, but he also lost everything (of material value) in the process.

SUMMARIZE: Hebrews 11:24-25 provides the scriptural commentary on this period of Moses' life. Note that Moses was not commended for attempting to deliver Israel. He was commended for making a definite choice. Which of the statements below would you say summarizes the result of Moses' commitment? (Choose one or more.)

His commitment benefited his people.

His commitment cost him material things.

His commitment cost him self-esteem.

His commitment was said by God to be an act of faith.

WHY IS COMMITMENT IMPORTANT TO THE LIFE OF THE BE-LIEVER?

Because God calls it an act of faith.

Because without commitment there can be no satisfactory growth.

2
Please Send Somebody Else!
Exodus 3-4

The first recorded dialogue between Moses and the Lord took place at a burning bush on the backside of the desert in Midian. Almost eighty years old at the time, Moses was doing what he had done every day for half of his life—tending his father-in-law's sheep. Noticing a strange bush that was obviously on fire, yet not being consumed, he went to investigate. When the voice of God spoke from the bush, Moses was brought face to face with a failure with which he had lived for forty years.

"I am the God of your father, of Abraham, of Isaac, and of Jacob," said the voice. "I have seen how my people are suffering in Egypt. I've heard them crying. I am going to deliver them." No one wanted freedom for Israel more than Moses, but he was unprepared for what the voice said next. "I'm sending you to Pharaoh to bring the Israelites out."

Suddenly somewhere within his being, Moses felt an old wound burst open and begin to throb. The memory of his abortive attempt to liberate Israel was as clear as if it had happened yesterday. He had gone so willingly to help. But he had failed. Instantly. Miserably. Completely. The Israelites were still slaves, and he had exchanged the comforts of the palace for nothing more than forty years of tending someone else's sheep.

Despite the fact that Moses had now worn shepherd's garb for as long as he had once worn royal robes, Midian was still not home to him. "A stranger in a strange land" he called himself. Wherever he lived, his identification would always be with God's people. He could not erase their plight from his mind. He walked in Midian's pastures but continued to see Egypt's brickyards. Above the sound of bleating sheep he seemed always to hear the distant sound of weeping slaves. He felt deeply for them. But past experience told him he was not the man for the job.

"Who am I?" he questioned God. "Who am I that I should go to Pharaoh?"

Who indeed? At eighty years of age, he was a prince without a palace. He was a man without a country. He was a shepherd without a flock.

It is hard to live with failure. It is even harder to attempt to do something at which you have already failed. In living with failure over a long period of time, one can amass a mountain of self-doubts. Picture yourself in Moses' sandals—forty years alone with nothing but your thoughts and all those sheep. Forty years in which to review everything you said and did in your one great attempt to do something for God. Forty years in which to convince yourself that you are most definitely not the one for the job. And then suddenly, unmistakably there is a summons to try again. "Go back to Egypt!"

What would be your reaction? "Who, me? What makes you think I am the man for this job?" Exactly! Moses' reaction was completely predictable, his reluctance to obey, completely understandable. And yet, from the beginning Moses should have understood that the burden of responsibility would not be resting on him.

In the dialogue at the burning bush, the Lord was very specific. Not only did He tell Moses who was to be the real deliverer (God) and who was merely the instrument (Moses), but God also told him who would listen to him (the elders of Israel) and who would not listen (Pharaoh). He told Moses what to say to Pharaoh, and He told him what would have to be done before Pharaoh released the Israelites. Moses, just as specific, interjected his doubts one by one. He doubted his calling. He doubted his credentials. He doubted his ability.

In response to Moses' first question, "Who am I that I should go?" God assured him, "I will certainly be with you." That might have been enough had it not been for the memory of someone's shouting at him, "Who made you a prince and a judge over us?" The thought of that began to sting again. This time, if there was to be a this time, Moses had to be sure of his credentials.

"Who shall I say sent me?" he questioned.

"Tell them the God of their fathers sent you. Tell them I said, 'I will bring you out of Egypt.' They'll listen to you."

"They will not listen!" argued Moses. (After all he had been that route before. He knew exactly what the reaction would be.) "They will never believe me," he continued. "They will say, 'The Lord hasn't appeared to you.' "

To placate Moses, the Lord gave three signs. His walking stick would become a snake. His hand would become leprous. Water from the river would become blood. Moses was to show those miraculous signs to the Israelite elders as proof that God had sent him as His instrument in an imminent deliverance.

Moses remained unconvinced. "What about my speech?" he prodded. "I'm slow. I can't speak convincingly, and Your talking to me hasn't changed that." It would seem that when God said, "I will be with you," He meant the whole person. Surely the "you" included the mouth. But just in case Moses had missed that point, the Lord spelled it out.

"Who made your mouth?" He demanded. "Who makes man to see, or hear, or speak? Haven't I done that? Now go on. I will be with your mouth!"

Still Moses had one more suggestion. "Lord," he pleaded, "please send someone else!"

The conversation ended as God, although angered with Moses, promised that Aaron would act as Moses' spokesman. And Moses went to Egypt.

The importance of Moses' action at that point can hardly be overemphasized. In a seemingly negative incident we find two very positive examples. Moses dealt with his doubts by facing them frankly and honestly. And Moses obeyed the Lord in spite of his personal feelings. From questions to arguments to pleading, Moses verbalized the fear and frustration he felt when confronted with an ostensibly impossible task. He knew exactly what God expected of him, but he did not think he could do it. He did not want to try. But he did. He left with us a vital lesson on obedience that is offered reluctantly. It is simply this. If you have nothing to offer the Lord except reluctant obedience, offer Him that.

It is enough.

It is a beginning.

Study Guide
HOW DOES THE BELIEVER FACE FAILURE AND DEAL WITH DOUBTS?
SCRIPTURE: Exodus 3:1—4:20

WHICH WOULD YOU RATHER DO? Assume responsibility for something you have never attempted or assume responsibility for something at which you have already failed? (Before going on with the lesson, think about and discuss that question briefly.)
HOW DID MOSES' PAST FAILURE AFFECT HIS RESPONSE TO GOD? Scripture Exercise, Part 1
   Read Exodus 3:1—4:13. Notice carefully all dialogue. Complete the following exercise.
Verse 6. How did the Lord identify Himself? _____

_____

Verse 7. What had the Lord seen and heard? _____

_____

Of what was He aware? _____
Verse 8. Who did God say would deliver Israel out of the hand of Egypt? _____ Who did He say would bring Israel into a land flowing with milk and honey? _____ It is obvious from this dialogue that God was to be the real deliverer. But He did have a task for Moses.
Verses 10-11. Circle the word that most accurately describes Moses'

reaction to God's command: (a) eager (b) confident (c) reluctant. Because Moses had already failed in that task, he had come to doubt his ability.

An unknown poet has expressed the truth that he who never doubted never thought. It is human to doubt, especially in light of past failure; however, if one is to grow in faith one must learn to deal with doubt. To discover how Moses dealt with his doubts, complete the following exercise.

HOW DID MOSES DEAL WITH DOUBT? *Scripture Exercise,* Part 2

You will note that Moses neither ignored nor denied his doubts. Instead, he verbalized them.

Verse 11 Moses asks _____

Verse 12 God answers _____

Verse 13 Moses asks _____

Verse 14 God answers _____

Verses 16-17. To whom was Moses to go first? _____

Verse 18. According to what God said, what would be the reaction of the elders? _____

Next, Moses was to go with the elders to the k _ _ _ of E _ _ _ _ _.

Verse 19. Was Moses told what the king's reaction would be? ____

Verse 20 emphasizes again that _____ was in control of the situation.

Compare 3:16-18 with 4:1, and note that Moses once again expressed his doubts. He could not accept God's promises because of that self-doubt. The Lord encouraged him again by giving him three signs. List those signs from 4:2-9. _____

Verse 10. What new doubt did Moses express? _____

Verse 12. How did God encourage him? _____

Verse 13. Was Moses then willing to go? _____

The Lord then promised to send Aaron as spokesman for Moses, and Moses arranged to return to Egypt (see verses 14-18).

SUMMARIZE: On the basis of this exercise how would you describe Moses' act of obedience in returning to Egypt? (a) wholehearted and enthusiastic (b) fully convinced that he was the man for the job (c) still reluctant and hesitant.

DOES RELUCTANT OBEDIENCE HAVE ANY VALUE? Yes, because it is a step in the right direction. An attitude of obedience is developed by obeying. Think of this: If children were permitted to obey only when they wanted to, they would never learn to obey. So it is with the believer. Obedience is learned by obeying, and the first step, however reluctant, is crucial.

3
God, Why Did You Bring Me Here?
Exodus 5-6

It was a great day in Egypt's land of Goshen when Moses and his brother, Aaron, came with their emancipation proclamation. Generations of Israelites had grown up in slavery. They knew nothing of freedom save what they had heard in the oft-repeated story of their ancestor Jacob. He had been a free man. Egypt had been kind to Jacob's family when he immigrated from Canaan because of the great famine. But that had been over four hundred years ago, and his descendants had long ago lost favor with Egypt's rulers. For much of the intervening time they had been slaves of the mighty pharaohs.

Even in bondage, Israel had maintained family and tribal structure. It was to the elders that Moses and Aaron delivered God's message and demonstrated the miraculous signs. Just as God had said, the elders listened and they believed. God had seen their suffering. He was going to liberate the slaves. Freedom was no longer to be just a word remembered from the past. Life was to be vastly improved because God had sent an emancipator. In anticipation of better days, the Israelites worshiped God on the spot, and Moses and Aaron proceeded to their confrontation with Pharaoh.

Then things got worse instead of better. Rumors of freedom were quickly succeeded by talk of a disturbing new development in the brickyards. Israelite overseers were being beaten because the slaves were no longer meeting their daily brick quotas. They were failing to meet the quotas because the straw supply had been cut off. In addition to making the bricks, the slaves were now responsible for the time-consuming task of gathering the straw used in the process. Yet they were required to meet their previous quotas. Just why the Egyptians had quit furnishing the straw, no one seemed to know.

It was from Pharaoh himself that the Israelite foremen got the official word on the straw situation. They went directly to him to lodge their protest.

"Why do you beat us?" they demanded. "No one gives us straw anymore, but your workmen yell at us, 'Make brick! Make brick!' We're not to blame. It's their fault!"

"You have too much time on your hands," accused Pharaoh. "That's why you say, 'Let's go sacrifice to the Lord in the wilderness.'"

So that was it! Suddenly the elders saw the situation very clearly. Moses and Aaron, the men who had come with such big promises, had actually precipitated the problem. They had angered Pharaoh by asking him for time off for the slaves.

"There will be no straw given," declared Pharaoh. "Now get out! See that you meet your quotas!"

With that impossible demand ringing in their ears, they left Pharaoh's court. Whom should they meet but the brothers themselves, the would-be liberators, Moses and Aaron.

"May God judge you for what you have done!" they shouted at Moses. "Because of you, Pharaoh hates us. Because of you, his servants have an excuse to kill us." The Israelites now understood that the promised deliverance was to have a price. Things were going to get worse before they got better. If anyone had considered the possibility that that was part of God's plan, it is not evident. It would seem that Israel wanted His deliverance, but not at such cost. It must be accomplished smoothly and with neither hardship nor inconvenience for them.

There were some things about the situation that Moses readily understood. God had told him the Israelite elders would listen. He had also told him that Pharaoh would not listen. But Moses had not known that Pharaoh's initial refusal would have such far-reaching effects. There had been no warning that the people he came to deliver would have to endure even more suffering before the liberation was accomplished.

There is a particular anguish known only by those who find themselves in a "why am I here?" situation. Moses knew he was exactly where God wanted him to be. Yet his very presence in that place had worsened the situation.

"Why, God? Why have You brought me here?" Moses poured out his heart to the Lord. "Why are You doing this to Your people? Ever since I came to Pharaoh to speak for You, he has mistreated them terribly. And You haven't delivered them at all!"

A pattern begins to take shape. The Egypt-to-Canaan drama is to be played against a background of contrasting reactions. The Israelites who instantly accepted God's purpose for their lives will totally reject His plan and His leader. Moses, his endless questions finally answered, will totally submit to God and to His plan. While Israel will constantly look for someone to blame, Moses will consistently look to God for help.

Sometimes help comes in the form of a reminder. Following the straw incident, Moses needed to be reminded that his responsibility was simply to obey and leave the rest to God. In a precise dialogue recorded in Exodus 6:1-8, God emphatically reminded him who was in control.

"You will see what I will do to Pharaoh," said the Lord.

"I am the LORD."

"I promised the land of Canaan to your forefathers."

"I remember my promise."

"I will deliver you."

"I will bring you to the land." Eighteen times in eight verses we read the pronoun "I." Obviously, God wanted to correct Moses' perspective. Until his eyes were diverted from circumstances, his heart would continue to cry, "Why, God?"

33

He was slow to learn. But he did learn. The record shows that that very dialogue became the foundation of Moses' unique rapport with the Lord. The promises given here were to become the very brick and mortar of an unparalleled relationship between one man and his God.

Study Guide
HOW SHOULD THE BELIEVER VIEW CIRCUMSTANCES?
SCRIPTURE: Exodus 5-6

HOW WOULD YOU HANDLE THIS SITUATION? A believer has prayerfully entered an area of service. He finds himself facing an unpleasant turn of events as a result. How should he view those circumstances in relationship to the Lord's leading in his life?
  A. The circumstances prove that he has taken a wrong turn in his life.
  B. The circumstances reveal that he has failed at the task.
  C. He should ignore the circumstances and praise the Lord anyway.
  D. He should look at circumstances as but one part of the total picture and should evaluate them in light of God's Word.

WHY DID CIRCUMSTANCES CAUSE MOSES TO QUESTION GOD'S LEADING IN HIS LIFE? Scripture Exercise

In the following exercise you will review some of those things that God had told Moses concerning the task before him, you will observe Moses' state of mind in Exodus 5:22-23, and you will reconstruct the events that led up to that point.

Exodus 3:7-8. At the burning bush God revealed to Moses that He (God) had seen _____

_____ and heard _____
and that He knew their _____. He further revealed that He (God Himself) would _____ them
out of the hand of the Egyptians and would _____
_____them to a land flowing with milk and
honey. God charged Moses with the task of going to Egypt, and
He promised Moses, "Certainly I _____
_____" (3:12). He also
promised him in 4:12 _____
_____.

Specifically Moses was charged to go to the elders of Israel. God
said, "They will _____" (3:18).
Moses was also to go to the king of Egypt. God said, "I am sure
_____" (3:19).
What else did God say concerning the king of Egypt's response?
(3:20) _____
_____

   In Exodus 5 we find Moses facing an unpleasant turn of events.
In your own words write the two questions that Moses asked God
(v. 22): (1) _____
_____ (2) _____
_____

What accusation did Moses make against God in verse 23? ___
_____

   Now reconstruct the circumstances preceding the action men-
tioned in those two verses. When Moses and Aaron went to the
Israelite elders (4:29-31), "Aaron _ _ _ _ _ all the words which
the _ _ _ _ had spoken unto Moses, and _ _ _ the _ _ _ _ _ in
the _ _ _ _ _ of the _ _ _ _ _ _." What was Israel's response to
the signs? _____
Was that response predictable (see 4:1 and compare with 4:8-9)?
_____ When Moses and Aaron went to Pharaoh (5:1-2) and
presented their request, what was Pharaoh's response?
_____ Do you think
that should have been a surprise to Moses? _____ Check your
answer against 4:21 and 3:19. Read verses 5:4-14 and describe

briefly what took place after Moses and Aaron went to Pharaoh.

_____

_____

When the Israelite elders presented their case to Pharaoh, he said, "Ye are idle [and that is why you say], Let us _ _ and _ _ _ _ _ _ _ _ to the _ _ _ _" (5:17). Whom did Israel blame for their predicament (v. 20-21)? _____ Why?

_____

Do you think Moses blamed himself (see 5:23)? _____

Which of the following statements do you think might explain why circumstances caused Moses to question God's leading in his life?

    A. Moses did not really want to help the Israelites.
    B. Moses was only interested in personal success.
    C. Moses did not remember God's words.

SUMMARIZE: To conclude the lesson taken from this event in Moses' life, it is essential that you discover how God diverted Moses' eyes from circumstances. Read Exodus 6:1-8 and count the occurrences of the pronoun "I" in those verses. In spite of present circumstances, God wanted Moses to understand that God was in control of the situation. He also explained to Moses that His purpose would be accomplished (a) quickly (b) overnight (c) with great judgment (see v. 6, 7).

THINK OF THIS: Someone has well said, "Never doubt in the dark what God has revealed in the light." The believer must always see circumstances as but one piece of the total picture and must always weigh those circumstances against God's Word. We are charged with a task. We must leave the results (and the circumstances) to God.

4
Look What Happened Tomorrow!
Exodus 7-12; Hebrews 11:27-28

The promises recorded in Exodus 6 were intended to give hope to the Israelites as well as to Moses. Moses was to deliver the message to the disillusioned slaves. But hope deferred makes the heart sick, and the Israelites were sick at heart. They did not want to hear about the God of their fathers. They did not want any promises about a land of their own or a divine Deliverer who would take them there. They had already concluded it was better not to hope. Then there would be no disappointment when freedom failed to materialize. They refused to listen to Moses. Not surprisingly, their reaction further discouraged Moses, who was still greatly concerned about immediate results.

Regardless of the Israelites' reactions, the Lord instructed Moses to go again to ask Pharaoh for Israel's release. Moses was reluctant. After all, the program was supposed to benefit the Israelites, and they wouldn't listen. Why should Pharaoh pay any attention to Moses? He was the big loser in the plan. "Look," Moses said to the Lord, "the Israelites haven't paid any attention to me. Why should Pharaoh listen?"

At that point the Lord gave Moses some important facts. There was more than deliverance involved there. Moses had been under the impression that all they were doing was releasing Israel from Egyptian bondage. And if that were all that was at stake, surely God could accomplish it differently. Quickly. Painlessly. But God now confided in Moses. "I will bring my people out by great judgments, and the Egyptians shall know that I am the Lord." There was a purpose in the delay. Israel's release was to be forced through great judgments that were intended to be a learning experience for Egypt and Israel alike.

The record shows that it was Moses himself who had the greatest learning experience. His perspective was definitely changed somewhere in the process of the judgments. It is obvious that he no longer cared about immediate results.

By the end of Exodus 9, a new Moses has emerged. We see Pharaoh bargaining with him over the hailstorm. "Pray to the Lord to stop it," he begs. "I'll let you go. You won't have to stay any longer." Moses agrees to pray, but then he looks Pharaoh in the eye and declares, "As for you, I know you will not do as you promised." He knew Pharaoh would not let them go, but that no longer mattered. Moses had come to see himself as a tool in the hands of a persistent, powerful God who was working daily miracles under the very nose of Pharaoh himself. All Moses had to do was follow instructions.

As Moses spoke, God turned the river to blood. Frogs infested the land. Dust became living, crawling lice. Flies swarmed over Egypt. Disease destroyed the livestock. Boils broke out on man and beast. Hail destroyed the crops. Locusts stripped away what was left. Thick black darkness enshrouded Pharaoh's kingdom. To Moses it was no longer important what other people did or did not do. God was definitely in control, and Moses was His instrument.

There were those in Egypt who did learn, even though their ruler remained obstinately blind. All Egypt watched as God drew a line between Goshen, Israel's habitat, and Egypt. What the Egyptians suffered, Israel was spared. Pharaoh's servants wisely pleaded, "Let them go before all Egypt is destroyed." From the common man to the ruling class, the Egyptians recognized Moses as a very great man. But Pharaoh refused to release the Israelites.

God explained to Moses that there would be one more judgment.

After that the Egyptians would thrust Israel out of the land. Before the final judgment took place, Pharaoh was amply warned. The firstborn of every household, man or beast, would die. Egypt would cry as she had never cried before. The people would beg Moses to leave and take the Israelites with him.

Israel would again be spared. But certain preparations had to be made. At God's command, Moses instructed the Israelites to kill a lamb, sprinkle the blood upon the doorposts, roast the lamb over the fire, and hold a feast. The Lord promised, "When I see the blood, I will pass over you." No one would die in the homes marked by the blood. Throughout history, generations of Jews have kept the Passover feast to commemorate the great deliverance from Egypt. That night in Egypt they kept the first Passover feast for the same reason—to commemorate their deliverance. There is one great distinction. The first time they celebrated, they were not yet delivered. On that night throughout the land of Goshen, slaves en masse slaughtered lambs and made strange bloody marks on their doorposts. They roasted the lambs over their fires, and then they celebrated an event that had not yet happened.

Moses is commended in Hebrews 11:27-28 for forsaking Egypt, not fearing the wrath of the king and for keeping (instigating) the Passover. God calls each act an act of faith. Moses clearly demonstrated faith in that case by taking God literally and acting on His word. God told Moses to keep the feast as an ordinance forever because on "this day have I brought you out of Egypt." "Brought" is past tense. When Moses instigated the Passover feast he believed the deliverance was an accomplished fact.

The impact of that is better felt when one examines both Exodus 12 and Hebrews 11. Every event referred to in Hebrews 11 is in strict chronological order. But the order is reversed in verses 27 and 28. Here, Moses is first commended for fearlessly forsaking Egypt and second for instigating the Passover. Because his flight to Midian could hardly be described as being without fear, we must assume that the final forsaking of Egypt is here indicated. Yet in Exodus 12 we see that the Passover feast came first, and then they left Egypt.

To commemorate an event before it takes place is like saying, "Look what happened tomorrow!" It is perceiving the promises of

God as accomplished facts even when circumstances belie those promises. Had Moses not believed deliverance was accomplished, he would have had no reason to keep the Passover feast. From faith's perspective, the forsaking of Egypt had taken place.

There was nothing left to do but celebrate.

OPEN BIBLE QUIZ

In place of a study guide for chapter four, the following open Bible quiz is offered. The purpose of the quiz is to enrich the student's understanding of God's judgments in Egypt. Although the average Bible student has a general knowledge of the plagues and the background of the Passover feast, very little attention is ever given to God's overall purpose in delivering Israel out of Egypt by means of judgments. The student who takes time to discover everything God said concerning His purpose in delivering Israel from Egypt in that manner will discover that more than the liberation of God's people was involved.

Instructions: Read the sentence and the corresponding Scripture references. Mark your answer "Agree" or "Disagree," or underline the word that correctly completes the sentence.

Agree Disagree

1. It is quite possible that God chose to deliver Israel by great judgments in order that the slaves could leave the country with ample material provisions (Exodus 3:19-22; 12:35-36). ____ ____
2. The miracles God performed while delivering Israel from Egypt were to be a means of teaching the Israelites that He was the Lord their God (Exodus 6:6-7). ____ ____

3. God also intended that those miracles be a means of showing Egypt that He was God (Exodus 7:4-5). _____ _____

4. Moses prayed for the deliverance of Egypt from the frogs because he thought that if he humored Pharaoh the Israelites would be allowed to leave (Exodus 8:8-10). _____ _____

5. God separated Goshen (Israel's habitat) from Egypt at the time of the judgment of the flies because He wanted to reward the Israelites for their faith in His plan (Exodus 8:20-22; 11:7). _____ _____

6. God was not trying to teach Pharaoh anything through the plagues (Exodus 9:13-14). _____ _____

7. God's victory over Pharaoh was one of the methods He used to declare His name throughout the earth (Exodus 9:16; Joshua 2:9-11). _____ _____

8. God's dealing with Pharaoh was intended to be a teaching tool for Israel's future generations so that they would know (a) how much the Israelites suffered (b) that Pharaoh was just a man (c) that God was the Lord (Exodus 10:1-2; 12:25-27).

9. God's wonders were multiplied in Egypt (a) when the people obeyed (b) when Pharaoh refused to listen (Exodus 11:9).

10. The route by which Moses led the Israelites out of Egypt was (a) unimportant as long as they got out (b) the shortest way out (c) chosen by God for the specific purpose of teaching the Egyptians that He was Lord (Exodus 14:1-4).

11. Israel escaped the plagues (a) permanently (b) temporarily (Exodus 15:26; 32:35).

12. Israel learned through observing what God did in Egypt (Numbers 14:11-12, 22-23). _____ _____

13. The magicians refused to recognize that God

was dealing with Egypt (Exodus 8:16-19). ____ ____

14. Some Egyptians were spared the judgments (Exodus 9:13, 18-21). ____ ____

15. Moses prayed for the Lord to stop the hail because he believed that Pharaoh would let the Israelites go (Exodus 9:27-30). ____ ____

16. Before the judgments ended, the servants of Pharaoh recognized the absolute power of God (Exodus 10:7). ____ ____

17. Moses, the man who had doubted his ability for the job, became elevated as a leader through the plagues (Exodus 11:3). ____ ____

18. Compare Exodus 12:29-36 with Exodus 3:19-22. Had God revealed to Moses how Israel would be delivered? ____ ____

19. God never intended Israel to live in Egypt for over four hundred years (Genesis 15:13; compare with Exodus 12:41). ____ ____

5

A Promise Is a Promise Is a Promise
Exodus 32-33

The final judgment came at midnight. In Egypt all was chaos. The usual quiet darkness had been displaced by thousands of flickering lights and a weeping unlike anything Egypt had ever experienced. In the palace, Pharaoh's son was dead. In every home in Egypt, the firstborn had died. Cattle lay dead in the pastures. And in the palace dungeon the prisoner received a message. "Your son is dead."

Pharaoh knew what he had to do. Hastily, he sent for Moses and Aaron. "Get up and get out of here," he ordered, "you and the Israelites. Go serve the Lord as you asked. Take your flocks with you. Get going!" And then he begged, "Bless me also." Fearing for their very lives, the Egyptians urged the Israelites to leave at once. In a mass evacuation, Goshen was emptied of some two million people. It was a night to be remembered. It was exactly 430 years to the day since Jacob's family had come to Egypt because of the great famine.

As was to be expected, when Pharaoh realized that his manpower was gone, he wondered out loud, "What have we done!" and led a great contingent of chariots to pursue Israel. The Israelites had camped at the Red Sea when Pharaoh caught up with them. Miraculously the sea parted, and Israel crossed on dry land. But the pursu-

47

ing Egyptians drowned. As has been previously pointed out, the Israelites were commended in Hebrews 11 for crossing the sea as God commanded. Their mental attitude was not indicative of the usual concept of faith, but they did obey. God deemed that act of obedience an act of faith. It could have been a beginning. But it wasn't.

The believer who desires to grow in faith would do well to remember that the children of Israel were commended for crossing the sea, but only Moses was commended for forsaking Egypt. Although the Israelites did sing a song of praise to God for their safe crossing, in less than three days the song was replaced by murmuring. In six weeks time they were saying, "We wish we had died in Egypt where at least we had plenty to eat."

Three months to the day after they fled Egypt, the Israelites set up camp at Mount Sinai. In that short time they had witnessed some miraculous provisions, they had begun their lifelong grumbling routine, and they had hastily promised that they would gladly do whatever God asked them to do. Between Egypt and Sinai, the cloud and the fire had guided them constantly; water, quail, and manna had been provided; Amalek had been defeated. Yet the people so recently removed from bondage had already complained bitterly against God: "Why did He bring us out here on this desert to die of starvation?"

After they camped at Sinai, God gave Moses a message for the people. Reminding them of His care in bringing them out of Egypt, God promised they would be His special people if they would obey Him. Instantly the Israelites declared, "Everything He says, we'll do!" The promise seems very rash for a people who had already begun to show signs of anarchy. But they were sure that all God had to do was spell it out and they could take care of the rest.

So the giving of the Law began. It was a lengthy process involving a final forty-day period during which Moses remained on the mountain with God. The people grew restless. They concluded that Moses was never coming back and that the God whom they had promised to obey was not there anymore. Impatiently they insisted that Aaron do something. "Make us gods to go before us," they demanded, "because we have no idea what has happened to that man Moses who brought us out of Egypt." Then Aaron, the spokesman whom Moses had been so sure he needed, collected all their golden ornaments, melted them, formed a golden calf, and proclaimed a feast day. The Israelites celebrated by eating, drinking, playing, and worshiping the idol they had proclaimed to be the god who had brought them out of Egypt.

Meanwhile, up on the mountain the Lord informed Moses of what was going on in camp.

"Go back down the mountain," He ordered. "Your people whom you brought out of Egypt have corrupted themselves. They have already forgotten everything I told them." Explaining to Moses that the people had made a golden calf, the Lord continued, "I've seen what these people are like—stiff-necked. Let Me alone and I will destroy them. In their place I'll make another nation of you."

There had been a time when Moses had hastily assumed responsibility for the Israelites. When he made that initial commitment to identify with God's people, he had assumed that he was to take care of the people himself. When he tried and failed, he could not face the prospect of trying again, because he still assumed the responsibility was his. But now Moses knew differently. Those were not his people. They were God's people. Moses had not delivered them. God had.

Moses remembered very well all the Lord had told him. Even at the burning bush in that first encounter the Lord had said, "I have seen the affliction of *my* people. *I* am come to deliver them." And then in that explicit conversation following the straw incident, God reiterated his promise to Abraham, Isaac, and Jacob. He also made abundantly clear that He was the divine Deliverer and Israel was *His* people. Moses recalled that God said, "Even Egypt will know that I am the Lord when I bring my people out from among them." In a rather subtle manner, Moses responded to the Lord's statement.

"Lord," he asked, "why are you angry with *Your* people, which *You* have brought out of Egypt?" He challenged, "Why should the Egyptians have a chance to say, 'He took them out to the wilderness to kill them and wipe them off the face of the earth'?" Moses also reminded God of His promise to Abraham, Isaac, and Jacob. "You swore to them to multiply their seed and give them the land." It is evident that the lessons Moses learned so slowly had been permanently implanted. He did not try to defend the people. Instead, he reminded God of the promises that had to be fulfilled. And he won his case. God did not destroy the people.

Recently I attended a convention at which a veteran missionary from Taiwan told about the Chinese word for "faith." He explained that the word is composed of two characters, the character for "man" leaning against the character for "word." Instantly I thought of Moses. From the instigation of the Passover to the end of his life, Moses appears to have literally leaned on the words of God. All those promises that he had seemed not to hear, surfaced to his conscious level. From the Exodus to his death at Pisgah, the daily dialogues reveal a man who boldly demonstrated his faith by simply reminding God of His promises.

Moses did not arrive at that point overnight. He began with a definite commitment. He made a choice. He turned his back on one thing in favor of something better. Then he faced his failures and doubts frankly. One by one he dealt with each problem. Then he obeyed God, even when he did not feel like it. From that beginning there grew a more complete obedience. Of necessity that obedience demanded an implicit trust on Moses' part. Only when he had learned so to trust could he then remind God that a promise is a promise is a promise.

The Chinese have a word for it!

Study Guide

HOW IS THE ABILITY TO STAND ON THE PROMISES OF GOD DEVELOPED?
SCRIPTURE FOR FURTHER READING: Exodus 32-33

DISCUSSION TOPIC: Some believers demonstrate a determination to stand on the promises of God regardless of circumstances. Other believers crumble under circumstances regardless of the promises of God. Which of the statements below would, in your opinion, explain that problem?
  A. If a believer knows the promises of God, he will stand on them.
  B. Only religious fanatics take the promises of God literally.
  C. If a believer sees the power of God demonstrated, he will be more apt to stand on God's promises.
  D. The believer who continually looks back to his old life will find it difficult to accept the promises of God.

WHY DID ISRAEL NEVER COME TO ACCEPT GOD'S PROMISES? Scripture Exercise

In the text, chapter 5 emphasizes Moses' progress in accepting the promises of God. For contrast, the study guide for this chapter will emphasize Israel's lack of progress. To give a picture of the nation's actions and reactions, chart the first three months out of Egypt as outlined below.

A. Choosing the route (Exodus 13:17-18; 14:1-4; 13:21-22)
   1. What was the shortest route? _____
     Why did God not allow the Israelites to go that way?
     _____

   2. What specific reason did God give for leading them into
     the wilderness before the sea? _____
     _____

   3. What immediate provision did He give them to lead
     them on their journey? _____
     Would you call that a demonstration of the power of
     God? _____
B. Response to God's deliverance from the pursuing Egyptians
  (Exodus 14:31; 15:1)
   1. Name two positive responses that Israel evidenced in
     14:31. _____
     _____
     _____

   2. What did the Israelites do to demonstrate their attitude
     toward their deliverance (15:1)? _____
     _____

C. Response to hardship
   1. How soon was Israel's song turned to murmuring
     (Exodus 15:22-24)? _____
   2. What was the occasion of that murmuring? _____
     _____

   3. When did the Israelites arrive in the wilderness of Sin
     (16:1)? _____
     _____

   4. What problem were they facing there (16:2-3)? _____
     _____

     In their murmuring at that point they specifically men-
     tioned God, Moses, and Egypt. In your own words write
     what they said. Use the following "starters" or, if you
     wish, form your own sentences.
     (a) I wish that God _____
     _____

     (b) At least in Egypt _____

(c) You (Moses) have _____

5. What miraculous provision was given in response to their need at that point (16:4, 11-15)? _____

6. Note that Moses repeated to the Israelites the lesson they were supposed to be learning (v. 6). What was that? The L _ _ _ hath _ _ _ _ _ _ _ _ _ _ _ _ _ _ from the _ _ _ _ of E _ _ _ _.

7. What warning did Moses give the Israelites concerning their murmuring against him and Aaron (16:8)?_____

8. At Rephidim (17:1) the people again accused Moses of bringing them out of Egypt to kill them, their children, and their cattle. Of what did they expect to die this time (17:3)? _____

9. To what degree had their anarchy progressed (17:4)? _

   In spite of God's miraculous provisions, what were the Israelites saying (17:7)? _____

10. God's answer to that complaint was to provide water from the rock in _____ (17:6). How was that accomplished (17:5-6)? _____

D. The first battle
   The Israelites faced their first warring enemy less than three months out of Egypt. That was _____ (17:8). Read 17:8-13, which describes the battle. Would you say the battle was won because (a) the people were trained in battle? (b) Moses knew battle strategy? (c) the Lord miraculously intervened?

E. The people respond to a challenge
   1. When did the people arrive at Sinai (19:1)? _____

      Now read 19:3-6 carefully and answer the next question.
   2. The first part of the message Moses was to give to Israel

was in the form of a (a) question (b) reminder (c) admonition (v. 19:4). Next, God said that the Israelites would be a p _ _ _ _ _ _ _ t _ _ _ _ _ _ _ unto Him above all people (v. 5). What was the condition of that promise (v. 5)? "If _ _ _ _ _ _ _ _ _ _ my _ _ _ _ _ indeed, and _ _ _ _ my _ _ _ _ _ _ _ _ _."

3. What was Israel's response to that challenge (v. 8)?) _ _

SUMMARIZE: On the basis of the preceding Scripture exercise you see that for the most part Israel's response was very negative even in the first three months; however a few positive responses were evidenced shortly after crossing the Red Sea. Which of the following statements are true?

A. When Israel saw what the Lord did to the pursuing Egyptians, they believed God and Moses.

B. Israel's record of trusting God would indicate that the nation had proved they could do whatever God asked.

C. Israel was commended for forsaking Egypt.

D. The Israelites sang praises to the Lord for delivering them from Pharaoh's armies.

DID ISRAEL EVER FORSAKE EGYPT? Acts 7:39 tells us that in their hearts the Israelites turned back to Egypt. Hebrews 11:27-29 tells us that the Israelites were commended for crossing the sea, but that only Moses was commended for forsaking Egypt. Turn back to the topic for discussion on the first page of this study. Reexamine the statements in light of the exercise you have completed. You will see that Israel demonstrated the truth of statement D and also showed that neither A nor C were always true. Are you failing to appropriate the promises of God because you are looking back with your heart?

6
If You're Not Going, Lord, Don't Send Me!
Exodus 32-33

At no time do we see Moses so tenaciously clinging to the promises of the Lord as in the days following the golden calf incident. In a conversation that spanned several days, he demonstrated a faith so bold it would neither cower, shrink, nor fear. His confidence was unshakable; his rapport could only be described as incredible.

When Moses came down from the mountain, he came face to face with reality. Any hope that Israel would learn to trust God was silenced by the thunder of dancing feet and drunken voices. He could expect no significant change in a people who, having witnessed so many miracles, would give deliberate obeisance to a metal monster. If he had dreamed of the day when they would demonstrate responses worthy of a freed people, he could now forget it. Theirs was a slave mentality, which would render neither cooperation nor enthusiasm. They would feel no loyalty to a leader, human or divine.

The incident proved to Moses that he was completely without human resources. Not only had the Israelites demonstrated that nothing could be expected of them, but Aaron also had failed him.

Appeasing the crowd had been his only concern. When Moses confronted him with his involvement, he denied it. "All I did was throw in the gold," he said, "and out came this calf."

Dependence upon the Lord is never so complete as that dependence that results from the knowledge that all human help is gone. There is a unique strength that comes to the believer when he perceives at last that there are no resources other than the promises of God. Unfortunately it is a lesson that must often be learned by experience. From the beginning, He who spoke from the bush had intended that Moses depend on no one but Himself. For the Speaker had known all along what Moses had now learned the hard way—Aaron, the talented orator, would crumble in a crisis.

While on the mountain, Moses had interceded for the people. Back in camp he dealt with their sin. He ground the golden calf to powder, sprinkled it on the water, and forced the people to drink it. At his orders 3,000 guilty were slain. Having judged the people's gross sin, he went again to pray for them.

His impassioned plea for forgiveness reveals the depth of Moses' identification with the people. His heart was breaking for them. Willing to be blotted out of God's book in exchange for their forgiveness, Moses pled with God for the people. It is in a dialogue following his prayer that we have a dramatic example of Moses' faith in action.

"Go on to the land," instructed the Lord. "You and *your* people that *you* have brought out of Egypt. I will send an angel before you and drive out the enemy." Then in a reversal of a prior promise, God continued, "I will not go up with you—you are a stubborn people, and I might consume you in the way." The conversation ended for the moment, but Moses refused to consider the issue closed. He was not willing to accept an angelic presence as a substitute for the divine Deliverer. On the strength of a prior promise he determined that he would not lead the Israelites anywhere unless the Lord Himself went in their midst. In spite of Moses' deep identification with Israel, he knew they were God's people and God's responsibility. He would bring the subject up again.

In the meantime Moses did tell the people what God had said. Even Israel recognized how precarious their position was when told the Lord would not go among them. Stripping themselves of their ornaments, they affected an attitude of repentance and waited. From their tent doors they worshiped, while at an appointed place outside the camp Moses communicated with God.

Simply, but frankly, Moses reopened the conversation.

"Look," he said, "You tell me, 'Bring the people up,' but You have not told me who is going with me—if it's really true that You know me by name and I have found grace in your sight, then tell me what You are going to do." And then as though to keep the record straight, he added, "And don't forget this nation is *your* people."

Faith frankly spoken produced the desired results. "I will go with you," replied the Lord, "and I will give you rest."

"If You're not going, Lord," Moses persisted, "don't send me!" Then he spoke what was on his heart. "How will anyone know that I and Your people have found grace in Your sight if You don't go with us? Only then can we be separated, I and Your people, from all the people of the earth."

There was something incredibly clear about Moses' perspective at that point. There was absolutely no confusion about resources, responsibilities, or relationships.Neither bravado nor audacity inspired him to communicate with God in that manner. Rather he was motivated by a frank assessment of his task and his position. He understood the immensity of his job. He knew precisely what was expected of him. He knew he was devoid of human resources. There was nothing left but the promises of God.

He needed nothing more.

He would settle for nothing less.

Study Guide
HOW DOES THE UNDERSTANDING OF GOD'S WORD AFFECT FAITH GROWTH?
SCRIPTURE: Exodus 32-33

DISCUSSION TOPIC: In our study thus far we have seen the value of commitment, of obedience, and of standing on the promises of God. To what extend does the understanding of God's Word affect the believer's ability to make a commitment, obey the Lord, or claim His promises? (a) not at all (b) very little (c) somewhat (d) quite a lot. Explain your reasoning.

HOW DID MOSES' KNOWLEDGE OF GOD'S WORDS TO HIM AFFECT THE GROWTH OF HIS FAITH? Scripture Exercise

1. Read Exodus 32:1-8. Describe the scene that was taking place back in camp while Moses was on the mount with God. _____

_____

_____

2. What two things did God say He was going to do as a result of the people's sin (v. 10)? _____

_____

_____

3. Moses presented three arguments against that announcement. Match the arguments with the verse in which it is found (11-13). Remember Your promise to Abraham, Isaac, and Jacob (Israel).

59

Why should the Egyptians say that You brought the people out here to destroy them? _____

Why are You angry with *Your* people? _____

4. On what do you think Moses based his reasoning with God?
   a. Education received in the palace
   b. Logic
   c. Prior promises of God
   d. Planning sessions with Aaron

   Note that Moses judged the people for their sins (19-28), and then he went to pray for them. Note the depth of his identification with Israel as he prayed for their forgiveness (32-33).

5. How does God's charge to Moses in 33:1-3 differ from the same charge given in previous dialogues? (a) Moses was not to take Aaron. (b) God said He would not go with them. (c) Moses was now to be responsible for driving out the enemy.

6. To help him in the task of leading Israel to the land, Moses, at one time or another, had each of the following resources. Circle the one resource that was left, and explain why you think he no longer had the others: (a) Aaron's assistance (b) the promises of God (c) God's very presence in the midst as they made the journey (d) Israel's belief in God and in Moses.

   Notice how Moses used the resource that he had left. Read 33:12-17. Moses reminded God of those things that God had said (promised) in the past.

7. What oft-repeated statement of the Lord did Moses bring up (v. 13)? The nation belonged to _____.

8. How important was it to Moses that God go with them to the land (v. 14, God speaking; v. 15, Moses speaking)? _____
   _____

SUMMARIZE: To chart the growth of Moses' faith thus far, arrange the following sentences in the order in which Moses might have spoken them.

   Lord, you are in control!
   Lord, I can't, I can't, I can't!
   Lord, why am I here?

60

Lord, You promised, You promised, You promised!
THOUGHT: Only as Moses came to understand God's words to him more thoroughly did he demonstrate faith that had grown to the heights seen in chapter 33.

7
Battle Fatigue, Complaints, and Critics
Numbers 11-12

Sometimes the urge to quit is overwhelming, especially when physical weariness is compounded by emotional conflicts. Great moments of victory are often followed by devastating periods of depression. Life itself becomes unbearable under a weight of responsibilities. In the final chapters of this book we will look at episodes from Moses' life that show faith under pressure. He experienced pressures common to all believers. Weariness, complaints, and criticism were his constant companions. The focus shifts in these dialogues. Here we shall view not how faith acts, but how faith reacts.

The dialogue in Numbers 11 reveals that a permanent plateau is never reached. Learning to lean on God's word does not preclude subsequent discouragement.

"Why did You do this to me?" Moses cried to the Lord. "Why should I be responsible for this people? Am I the father of all these people? Do I have to carry them like babies all the way to the land You promised?" The going was getting rough. Everyone was tired. They had just completed a three-day walk. It was the first journey since camping at Sinai. It was the very first time they had marched in precise order as prescribed in the Law. Unfortunately, order in marching did not guarantee order in camp. Weariness heightened other complaints. Originating with a few aliens and quickly taken up by the Israelites, their complaints pointed to a monotonous diet, and of course, as had become customary, to the good old days in Egypt.

"Remember how it was!" they lamented. Egypt was fifteen months behind them. Their memory was becoming increasingly selective. Slavery was long forgotten. Egypt had now become the personification of all things of which they were deprived.

"We had plenty of fish. All we wanted!"

"And melons."

"And don't forget the onions and garlic!"

"We want meat!"

"All we see is manna, manna, manna. We're sick of it."

They were sick of manna. Moses was sick of them. He spread his despondency before the Lord.

"If this is the way it's going to be, let me die now," he said. "Where can I get meat for these whining people? God, I can't bear this responsibility by myself. It's too much!"

Nothing is so energy-sapping as dealing with complaints, especially to the already weary. Whether a leader with sulky subordinates, a laborer with cantankerous coworkers, or a mother with cranky children, endless complaints can be debilitating. Isn't it good to know that God is concerned about weariness? He understood Moses' need. He encouraged Moses by giving him helpers. The Lord instructed Moses to choose seventy men. It is worth noting that God said two things of those men. First, they were to be men in whom Moses had confidence. After all, they were to assist him. Second, God promised to spiritually equip the men for the job. Any leader should find encouragement from that combination.

Having taken care of Moses, the Lord turned His attention to Israel. The complaining, ungrateful, liberated slaves were to have their meat. "Prepare yourselves," God ordered. "Tomorrow you will have meat! You think you had it so good in Egypt—you want meat—I'll give you meat until it's coming out of your noses! You'll have meat for one whole month. You'll have meat until you're sick of it." Then disclosing His reasoning, He concluded, "You have despised me, and you have cried, 'Why did we leave Egypt?' "

The provision of meat was used as an occasion to teach the Israelites the importance of obedience and unity. Once again, Israel witnessed the removal of the guilty from their midst as the greedy were stricken with the plague and died. But Israel did not learn by God's judgment any more than she learned by His mercies. Throughout their wilderness experience, the people reacted incorrectly in every situation because they were totally oblivious to what God was doing in their midst.

Miriam and Aaron were the next to disrupt the camp. Like all the Israelites, they were slow to learn. Witnessing God's punishment did not impress them as it should have. Their whisper campaign was directed against Moses. They did not like his wife. And they resented his position. "Has God only spoken by Moses?" they asked. "Hasn't He also spoken by us?" That seems a remarkable conclusion coming from the man who had fashioned the golden calf. Israel's worship of the calf had brought plagues upon her (Exodus 32:35). It had prompted the Lord to say, "I'll destroy these people." Moses had been the one who had pleaded for their forgiveness. He had willingly offered his life for theirs. "But God speaks through us too," Miriam and Aaron said. "Moses isn't the only one."

Perhaps leaders more than laymen are most vulnerable to that type of criticism. When attacking a leader, for lack of anything more specific, it always seems convenient to criticize his wife or accuse him of having too much pride. ("He thinks he's the only one through whom God can speak.") But there is a lesson here for all of us as we examine Moses' reaction to the criticism. He said nothing. He remained silent as God took charge of the situation. Upon hearing the criticism from Miriam and Aaron, God spoke to all three of them and commanded them to come out to the appointed place to listen to Him. Singling out Miriam and Aaron, He then said:

"Listen to me now! If there is a prophet among you, I speak to him in visions and dreams. But with Moses it is different. I speak very plainly to him. He will see my very likeness. You should be afraid to speak against my servant Moses."

Clearly, the Lord was very angry with Miriam and Aaron. When He withdrew His presence, Aaron looked at his sister and to his

65

dismay saw that she was leprous. Recognizing the seriousness of their sin, a penitent Aaron confessed their need of forgiveness, and Moses prayed to God to heal his accuser.

To be the object of criticism is never easy. Handling it demands discernment. This incident is not meant to teach that there is only one way to handle criticism. On the contrary, in subsequent incidents Moses responded to his critics very vocally and very boldly. Circumstances and the nature of the criticism must always be considered. In this case, Moses was being accused of spiritual pride. Envy had grown in the heart of the sister who had once watched as the infant brother was plucked from the Nile. She who had played such an important part in his destiny somehow resented his position as her leader.

Many believers, lay people as well as leaders, must face that type of pressure at sometime or another. Just like Moses, you find yourself doing your best to do a job that you never asked for in the first place. You have finally learned the hard way that it is the Lord's work, and you are but an instrument. You are completely dependent on your relationship with the Lord to get you through one day at a time. Then suddenly from where it is least expected, criticism comes. "He (she) thinks he's (she's) so great! The Lord uses me too!" What should be the reaction of a mature faith?

Against the criticism of spiritual pride, there is very little defense. Some private heart-searching may be in order. One must determine that there is no truth in the accusation. In Moses' case, the Holy Spirit explicitly declares the accusation to have been groundless. It is mandatory that the criticism be definitely committed to the Lord. The believer may rest assured that the Holy Spirit is able to work in hearts that refuse to be changed by human reasoning. Finally, a mature faith always leads the believer to pray for his accusers. Such a believer knows with certainty that the Lord takes care of His own. He acts—and reacts—accordingly.

Study Guide
HOW SHOULD A MATURE FAITH REACT TO DAILY STRESS AND PROBLEMS?
SCRIPTURE: Numbers 11-12

HOW WAS YOUR DAY? Which of the following might affect the way you react to a situation on any given day? (Choose one or more.)

A. Physical weariness

B. Mental fatigue

C. Weight of responsibility

D. Relationship with people involved in the situation

Scripture Exercise

1. Chart the complaints that Moses faced in Numbers 11-12. Read the reference, isolate the complainer(s) and the topic of the complaint, and list in appropriate columns.

Reference	Complainer(s)	
Numbers 11:4-6	(1) m _ _ _ _	
	m _ _ _ _ _ _ _ _	_____
	(2) C _ _ _ _ _ _ _ of	
	l _ _ _ _ _	_____
Numbers 11:10	(3) e_ _ _ _ m _ _	_____
Numbers 12:1	(4) M _ _ _ _ _ and	(v. 1) _____
	(5) A _ _ _ _	(v. 2) _____

2. Moses spread his problem before the Lord (11:10-15). What was his attitude toward the people's complaints (v. 10)? _____

_____

He made the following statements recorded, in modern vernacular, in 11:11-15. Mark beside each statement the verse in which it is found.
a. Why are You doing this to me? _____
b. Am I the father of these people? Must I carry them like babies to the land You gave them? _____
c. How can I give these whiners what they want? _____
d. I simply can't do this job all by myself! _____
e. Lord, if You really love me, take me to be with You and get me out of this mess. _____

We must assume that this was a case of sincere discouragement, an "end of the rope" type of problem with Moses. God graciously answered his cry and eased the load. Note that Moses was to choose the men who were to help him (v. 16) and that God would place His spirit upon them (v. 17) so that they would help Moses bear the burden of the people. God also answered the complaints of the Israelites, but in the process He judged those who had complained the most.

3. What specific reason did God give for judging Israel at that point (11:18-20)? _____

_____

4. What are some of the possible underlying factors behind Miriam and Aaron's second complaint (12:2)?
a. They were accusing Moses of spiritual pride.
b. They were accusing Moses of taking upon himself too much authority.
c. They were accusing Moses of paying too little attention to his family.
d. They were tired of taking a back seat.

5. Do you feel that a believer who finds an area of service is vulnerable to any of those problems? _____ Explain your answer. _____

_____

The Scripture does not give any indication that Moses attempted to answer the accusation made by Miriam and Aaron. Instead it reveals what God said. How is Moses described (12:3)? _____

6. Read 12:4-8 and summarize what God told Aaron and Miriam.

_____

7. How did Moses react to Aaron's confession of wrongdoing (12:11-13)? _____

8. Read Matthew 5:44 and copy the portion of the verse that was demonstrated by Moses on that occasion. _____

SUMMARIZE: Which of the following principles would you say are demonstrated in that incident from Moses' life?
   A. Take your discouragement to the Lord.
   B. Always defend yourself if you are in the right.
   C. Pray for those who do you wrong.
   D. Commit difficult accusations to the Lord.
   E. Never get involved with people.
Have you learned to take daily stress and problems to the Lord?

8
Miracles, Mercies, and Myopia
Numbers 13-14

"How long will it be before these people believe me for all the signs and wonders which I have done?" That rhetorical question posed by the Lord in Numbers 14:11 points to the progression of Israel's unbelief. All the wonders from Egypt to Kadesh had gone unheeded. Neither miracles nor mercies had inspired them to trust in the Lord. Disobedience was compounded by refusal to acknowledge it. Making excuses and shifting blame led to more disobedience. Punishment for disobedience only resulted in more excuses and more blame shifting. Continual disobedience sears the conscience, clouds the perspective, and distorts the reasoning. Irrepressible rebellion was inevitable.

There is an inescapable lesson to be drawn from the parallel examples of Israel and Moses. Through a series of actions and reactions one may become characterized by obedience or by disobedience. Moses' faith grew in direct proportion to his obedience. That which began as hesitant trust progressed to unshakable confidence because the more he obeyed God the more he trusted Him. By contrast, that which begins as instant belief can digress to obstinate unbelief. Israel's initial reaction to God's purpose for the nation was that of instant acceptance. The elders believed God and worshiped

(Exodus 4:31). But when the going got rough, Israel rejected God's plan in total. Her single act of obedience (Hebrews 11:29) could have been a beginning. Instead, from that point on it was downhill all the way.

By the time they camped at Kadesh-barnea, Israel was so characterized by disobedience that her reactions were entirely predictable. There on the very threshold of the promised land, Israel's disobedience gave rise to a full-scale rebellion. While camped at Kadesh-barnea they organized a reconnaisance unit to search out the land. The unit was composed of twelve men, carefully chosen from among the rulers of each tribe. Their orders were simple. Look at the land. Is it good or bad? Is it productive? Is there wood? Look at the people. Are they strong? Weak? Few? Many? Do they live in fortified cities? In tents? They were requested to bring back samples of the fruit, and finally they were admonished to be courageous. Clearly and simply they were charged with bringing back a report. No recommendation was requested. None should have been given. Of the twelve, only Caleb and Joshua carried out the orders as intended.

After forty days the spies returned with a report and a recommendation by ten of them to forget the whole undertaking. "The people are too strong. They are gigantic. We are like grasshoppers to them. We'll never be able to take the land." Seeing the fear and panic that dire message was causing, Caleb tried to encourage the people. "We are well able to take them. Let's go!" But no one wanted to listen to the minority report. Right or wrong, the majority usually rules.

That was a bad night for Israel. They cried and mourned and murmured. Soon they became desperate. They wished they were dead. They could not understand why God had brought them out into that wilderness. They were sure they could never protect their wives and children from what lay ahead. What began with a negative report now climaxed with a decision to return to Egypt. "Let's choose a captain to lead us," they screamed. "Let's go back to Egypt." Outvoted or not, Caleb and Joshua felt a responsibility to the people. While Moses and Aaron prayed, Caleb and Joshua tried to restore order. Tearing their clothes, they stood up before the mob and reminded them of one important fact. If the Lord was with Israel, the enemies, however gigantic, were defenseless. "Don't rebel against the Lord," they pleaded. "Don't be afraid of the people." But Israel refused to listen. "Stone them, stone them!" they shouted. It was at that point that the Lord intervened and asked Moses, "When will they ever learn?" He continued, "I'll kill them with pestilence. I'll disinherit them. I'll make a greater nation of you."

One has to visualize the scene in order to appreciate Moses' reply. There he was, leading a people who refused to be led. After two years of whispering and complaining, they had openly challenged his leadership and adamantly refused to go on. The prospect of being relieved of such people could hardly be regarded as anything other than a personal panacea. But long ago Moses' thoughts had ceased to be for himself. Now his concern was for the Lord's great name and for the Lord's wandering people. "If you destroy these people, then Egypt and the other nations will say the Lord wasn't able to bring them to the land, so he killed them in the wilderness." He pleaded with God to show His great mercy once again and forgive His sinning people.

Although Israel was spared, they paid a terrible price for their rebellion at Kadesh-barnea. They were sentenced to wander in the wilderness one year for every day the twelve had searched out the land. Forty years they would spend in the wilderness. "Tomorrow," the Lord directed Moses, "turn around and go to the wilderness by the Red Sea. Tell the people what I say: 'Your carcasses shall fall in the wilderness, and all of you from twenty years old and upward will die there. Your children, whom you were so sure would be killed in the land, them will I bring in, and they will have the land that you have despised.' " Caleb and Joshua were assured that they would one day enter the land because of their faithfulness to the task that God had given them.

Upon hearing what was to happen, the Israelites began to cry once more. All night they wept and plotted. In the morning, they came to Moses with their latest decision. "Here we are," they declared, "We'll go to the place that the Lord promised. We were wrong." That time it was Moses' turn to wonder when Israel would

learn. "You are disobeying the Lord," he warned. "It won't work."
To do the right thing at the wrong time—that also is sin. The willful
Israelites insisted on going ahead, but, just as Moses had predicted,
they were driven back by their enemies.

An old adage states that there is none so blind as he who will not
see. Israel stands as an example of that truth. Caleb and Joshua
learned. Observing the same miracles as all of Israel, those two had
concluded that the Lord was worthy of their trust and obedience.
Neighboring nations had learned. The fame of Israel's God had
spread as the people were led through the wilderness by the divine
pillar. Those nations had concluded that something extraordinary
was going on in Israel's camp, and that God was there. But Israel
refused to learn. Neither miracles nor mercies could effect a cure for
her myopia.

Study Guide

REVIEW: ISRAEL'S DOWNHILL ROUTE TO REBELLION

Kadesh-barnea marks the end of God's patience with the Israelites. It was here that He decreed that all those over twenty years of age would never enter the land.

The following questions review the steps in Israel's route to full-scale rebellion.

1. The Israelites obeyed God in crossing the Red Sea. God called that _____.

2. How did Israel's obedience at the Red Sea contribute to the judgment of her enemies? _____

_____

3. When Israel saw what God did to the Egyptians, the people _____ the Lord and _____ the Lord and _____ _____ _____ (Exodus 14:31).

4. The people sang praises to the Lord for _____

_____(15:1).

5. The Lord promised to keep the people from the diseases of the Egyptians if they would (15:26) (a) keep clean (b) obey Him (c) follow the pillar of fire.

6. The Israelites suffered the plagues of the Egyptians because they
_____(32:35).

7. Through the provision of manna God said the Israelites were to
see that He was "the L _ _ _ y _ _ _ G _ _" (16:12). He gave
instructions regarding gathering manna: five days a week they
were to gather what they could eat and save nothing for morning. On the sixth day they were to gather enough for two days.
On the seventh there would be no manna given. How did the
Israelites disobey those instructions (16:19-20, 27-28)? _____

_____

8. Although Israel promised to do whatever God instructed the
people to do (19:8), what happened even before He finished
giving the Law to Moses (32:3-4)? _____

9. What was God's comment concerning the Israelites' lack of
obedience (32:8)? _____

_____

10. Having come to the very entrance of the land at Kadesh-barnea,
and having sent twelve men to spy out the land, why did Israel
not make plans to enter (Numbers 13:26-33)?

_____

11. Do you think their fears were justified? _____ Why, or why
not? _____

12. Who encouraged them to go in (Numbers 13:30)? _____

_____

13. What desperate move did the Israelites decide to take (Numbers
14:4)? _____

14. When Moses, Aaron, Joshua, and Caleb tried to stop them, what
was the people's response (Numbers 14:10)? _____

_____

15. Why should the people have believed God (14:11)? _____

_____

16. One complaint the Israelites registered was that their
w_____ and their c_____ would die in the
wilderness (14:3). How did God answer that complaint, which

actually intimated that He was not able to take care of the people (14:30-31)? _____

_____

17. What was the end result of Israel's rebellion (14:32-35)? _____

_____

18. Thought for discussion: How might the course of the Israelites have been changed?

9
The Disobedient Are Dispensable
Numbers 16

It takes but the most cursory study of Israel's wilderness wanderings to convince one that the very survival of those people depended on their obedience to Jehovah. What did that downtrodden mass of humanity know about self-government? Or self-preservation? Or warfare? They had been slaves for more than a dozen generations.

Where once the will to live had meant pitting oneself against Pharaoh's abuses, now it meant pitting oneself against that trackless wilderness in the never-ending search for food, refuge, and water. If the Israelites refused to obey the orders to march when the strange cloudy pillar began to move, how would they know where to go? If they refused to follow God's specific strategy in battle how could they expect to win? In His plan, God had thought of Israel's every need. Even their rules of sanitation were written into the divine Law to preserve them from disease. Survival was no problem so long as the people listened to God and kept His Law.

Because obedience was imperative, it is easily understood why judgment—prompt and severe—was necessary in cases of disobedience. Any move toward mutiny had to be repressed, not simply to protect Moses' authority or to insure reverence for Jehovah, but to protect the people themselves. Under mob rule, God's plan would quickly be supplanted by man's ideas. Without a leader, chosen and prepared by God, Israel could not long survive.

Throughout his experience with the Israelites, Moses' leadership was constantly subjected to criticism. Often it was openly challenged. Although God severely judged the guilty in each case, it seemed that nothing could deter Israel's bent to rebellion. Although the terrible finality of God's judgment at Kadesh-barnea changed the immediate goal of the nation, it did not change their nature. There were many uprisings subsequent to the experience at Kadesh-barnea.

One of the most severe was instigated by Korah, of the tribe of Levi, along with three men of the tribe of Reuben. Recorded in Numbers 16, it is particularly significant because of the intensity with which the people determined to have the last word. Korah, along with 250 well-respected men of the congregation staged a protest meeting against Moses and Aaron, saying, "You take too much authority upon yourself. All of this congregation is holy, every one of them. The Lord is with them all, so why do you put yourself above them?" Not only were those men challenging Moses' authority, but they were also seeking the priestly duties assigned to Aaron. After prostrating himself, Moses gave them a plan whereby they would know whom God considered to be holy. Each was to bring a censer of burning incense to offer the Lord the next day. Aaron would do likewise. God would choose who was His, and that one would be holy.

Moses also reprimanded Korah, reminding him that God had chosen the Levites out of all the congregation to minister in the Tabernacle to the congregation. "Isn't that enough?" Moses asked. "Must you have the priesthood too?"

Two of the ringleaders, Dathan and Abiram, were sulking in their tents. Moses sent for them, but they refused to come. Their reply to Moses was both impudent and ludicrous. "Isn't it enough that you brought us out of a land that flows with milk and honey to kill us in this wilderness? Must you also make yourself a prince over us? Furthermore you haven't brought us to a land that flows with milk and honey or given us the fruit of the land. What will you do—put out the eyes of all these men? We won't come up." Egypt, where Israel had cried under Pharaoh's whip, where Israel's children had died by Pharaoh's decree, where Israel's spirit had been broken by hard bondage, that same Egypt was now romanticized by Dathan and Abiram as a land of milk and honey. And Moses, as in an echo from the past, was once again accused of making himself a prince over Israel.

By the time the 250 men came the next day, bringing their censers of incense, Korah had gathered the entire congregation around his cause. It appeared that the mutinous leaders had won their place with Israel and Moses and Aaron were left completely alone. Then the glory of the Lord appeared, and the Lord spoke to Moses and Aaron. "Get out away from this congregation," He said, "so that I might consume them this instant." But Moses and Aaron prostrated themselves and cried, "O God, God of all our spirits, will you be angry with the whole congregation because of one man's sin?" In answer to their prayer, the Lord instructed, "Tell the congregation to get away from Korah, Dathan, and Abiram."

The people separated themselves, and then Moses challenged all of them. "Here is how you will know that the Lord sent me to do all these things, and that I haven't done anything of myself. If these men die a common death, then the Lord has not sent me. But if the Lord makes a new thing, and the earth opens her mouth and swallows them and everything that belongs to them, you'll understand that these men have provoked the Lord."

As he finished speaking, an earthquake swallowed up the ringleaders and all their possessions. The people, panic-stricken, ran from the sight, fearing that they too would be swallowed up. Fire destroyed the 250 men with censers, and God ordered the censers made into a covering for the altar as a reminder to Israel that no one other than Aaron's descendants should take upon themselves the ministry of the priesthood.

Despite the divine judgment, the people refused to believe that Korah and his cohorts had provoked the Lord. The very next day all the congregation came again to Moses. Unbelievably they now accused, "You have killed the people of the Lord."

Instantly the glory of the Lord appeared and He spoke to Moses and Aaron, "Get away from these people so I may consume them at once." Moses and Aaron prostrated themselves, and this time Moses knew that the offense was so great that judgment was to be instantaneous. Already people were dying. "Go quickly," he instructed Aaron. "Take a censer of coals from the altar, take incense, and go to the congregation and make an offering for them. The plague has already begun." As Aaron took his place between the living and the dead, the plague was stopped, but the disobedience that began with one man had cost the lives of fifteen thousand people. The contention had spread like a malignant growth until the destruction of the guilty became mandatory for the survival of the nation.

Even in face of judgment, Israel remained totally insensitive to what God was doing in her midst. Only Moses understood. He knew that God had a marvelous plan for Israel. And he alone understood that in God's plan the disobedient are always dispensable.

Study Guide

HOW DID GOD SHOW HIS LOVE THROUGH PUNISHMENT?
SCRIPTURE: Numbers 16

DISCUSSION TOPIC: Why does God want our obedience?
   A. *Only* because obedience shows reverence to Him
   B. *Only* because He knows what is best for us
   C. Both of the above
   D. Neither of the above
EXERCISE 1: Questions based on the first two paragraphs of chapter 9 in the text
   1. On what did the very survival of Israel depend? _____
   2. What part did obedience play in the following very practical areas of need?
      a. Finding a route through the wilderness _____
      _____
      b. Fighting warring enemies _____
      _____
      c. Keeping well _____
      _____
   3. What preparation did Israel have for self-rule? _____
   4. (Review question) In their attempt to rule themselves what are some of the things the people did?

a. They tried to return to _____ before crossing the Red Sea.
b. They worshiped _____ _____ _____.
c. They refused to enter the _____.
d. They chose a captain to lead them back to _____.
e. They insisted on going up to the _____ after God sentenced them to wander in the _____.
f. They demanded co-rule with _____.

EXERCISE 2: Scripture
1. The instigators of the rebellion in Numbers 16 were (v. 1) K _ _ _ _, D _ _ _ _ _ _, and A _ _ _ _ _.
2. How many men did they gather with them (v. 2)? _____
3. Those men were (a) common people (b) respected leaders (c) mixed multitude.
4. Read verse 3. In your own words write what the men said about (1) Moses: _____

_____

_____ (2) the congregation: _____

_____

5. Neither complaint should have been made if Israel had learned by past experience. Discuss why the remark concerning the congregation was foolish in light of the incident at Kadesh-barnea.

_____

Read again regarding Miriam and Aaron in chapter 12. Do you think what God said and did at that point should have prevented such accusations as were made against Moses in 16:3? _____ Why or why not? _____

_____

6. What accusations did Dathan and Abiram make in 16:12-14?
a. They called Egypt a land of m _ _ _ and h _ _ _ _.
b. They accused Moses of making himself a p _ _ _ _ _ over them.
c. They blamed Moses for not taking them to the l _ _ _.

7. How far did the rebellion of Korah spread (v. 19)? _____

_____

8. Why was not the entire congregation destroyed (vv. 21-24)? _

_____

9. What two things was Israel supposed to learn through God's judgment against the leaders of this uprising?
   a. The Lord had sent _____ (v. 28).
   b. The leaders of the rebellion had provoked _____
   _____(v. 30).
10. By what means were the men punished (vv. 31-33)? _____

_____

11. In spite of the severity of the punishment and the specific lesson they were to learn, what did the congregation do on the following day (v. 41)? _____

_____

12. What immediate judgment did God send (vv. 45-48)? _____

_____

13. How many people died as a result of this incident instigated by three men (v. 49)? _____

SUMMARIZE: In order to bring the children of Israel to the land, two things were necessary: they had to be kept alive, and they had to move from one place to another. Keeping them alive involved provision of food and water, sanitation laws, and battle strategy. God provided for all of that. Moving from Egypt to Canaan involved (1) direction (provided by the pillar of cloud and fire), (2) organization for marching (provided for in the Law), and finally (3) keeping down all anarchy, which kept them from following their leader. Thus even in punishment God showed His love for the people.

WHY DOES GOD WANT OUR OBEDIENCE? Because that shows our love and our reverence for Him, but also because He knows what is best for us.

10
The Last Word
Numbers 20, 27; Deuteronomy 1:37; 3:23-26; 33-34

No book concerning Moses would be complete without a chapter on Numbers 20, where there is found a sobering account of his disobedience at Meribah. Here the reader is abruptly reminded that Moses, after all, was made of mortal clay. He grew impatient. He lost his temper. He sinned. On many occasions Moses had observed the judgment of the Lord. At Meribah, he experienced it.

The incident, like a dozen others, began with Israel's reaction to privation. There was no water. As was always the case, they blamed Moses and Aaron. Coming together before Moses, the people began to quarrel with him.

"We wish to God we had died with the rest of the people."

"Why did you bring us into this wilderness so that we and our children could die?"

"Why did you force us to leave Egypt?"

"This is a terrible place. There is not a thing growing here, and there isn't any water to drink."

Although Moses and Aaron deliberately sought the Lord's instruction at that point, they then failed to carry through.

"Stand before the rock," God said, "gather all the camp, and before their eyes, speak to the rock. It shall give water." They did gather the congregation, but then Moses succumbed to an "I'm fed up to here with you" attack. Angrily he struck the rock and reprimanded the people.

"Listen here, you rebels," he shouted. "Must we fetch you water out of the rock?"

The water came. So did the word of the Lord. "Because you didn't believe me," God said, "to sanctify me in the peoples' eyes, you will not bring this congregation to the land which I have given them." It is from Moses' submission to that judgment that we draw our final lesson. The incident at Meribah teaches us that even in failure the believer can be victorious when he submits to God's discipline. It also forcefully illustrates that by submission, bitterness is avoided.

Certainly to our finite minds there were all the ingredients for a large case of bitterness there. Moses gave of himself unselfishly, unconditionally, and unceasingly for Israel's cause. In return he was misunderstood, maligned, and mistreated in Israel's camp. He deeply desired to enter the land. Israel despised the land. On innumerable occasions Moses had shown patience and self-control. On one he lost his temper and disobeyed God. Not once had Israel ever demonstrated an ounce of self-control or patience. They had disobeyed God many times. Moses was sincerely repentant over his sin. Israel was obstinately unrepentant. Why should Moses be forbidden to go to the land that the ungrateful Israelites would possess?

Moses had no such problems of perspective. He knew he was not judged on the basis of whether he did better or worse than the Israelites. He was judged on whether or not he obeyed the Lord. And at Meribah he did not. Experience with Israel had taught him that judgment for sin was inevitable. But it was a bitter disappointment. He pleaded with God to rescind the judgment. "O Lord, you have begun to show your servant your great name. Who is a God like you in all the heavens and earth who can do what you do? I beg you, let me go over to this great land." Moses later told the Israelites of the conversation (Deuteronomy 3:23-28). In recalling the prayer he informed the people, "The Lord was angry with me, and He said, 'Enough. I don't want to hear any more about it.' " Moses understood that when God said, "Enough," the matter was settled. The subject was closed. He would most certainly die before Israel entered the land.

The book of Deuteronomy completes the story of Moses' life. Variously known as his swan song, his sermon on the Law, or a summary of the Pentateuch, it is in fact a chronicle of Moses' submission to God's judgment at Meribah. Although the book concerns his final task of preparing the people for entry into the land, it is more than a record. It is a mirror of Moses' emotions as he went about his task. And it reveals a man who was totally devoid of bitterness. The evidence of his submission to Jehovah permeates the entire book. Apart from Meribah, I never fully appreciated the message of Deuteronomy. Against its background, Deuteronomy became a very awesome book. It is human nature to be bitter. When a long-sought-after goal is snatched away, the emotional trauma is so great that it becomes almost impossible to function. To train someone "less worthy" to reach that goal is not possible within the realm of human resources. Human nature says, "I quit!" Man's rationale says, "Unfair!" For many a believer, Meribah is where it all ends. For Moses, it was simply another beginning.

His first reaction upon learning that God's decision was final was concern for the people. "Let the Lord appoint a man over the congregation," he prayed, "that they will not be like sheep without a shepherd." Joshua was appointed to succeed Moses, and it became Moses' task to prepare the future leader as well as the people. In Deuteronomy we read Moses' instructions, his encouragement, his warnings, his blessings, and his prophecies, all spoken to a people going to a land into which he could not enter.

A bitter spirit would certainly have viewed Israel as the constant source of heartache that she was. But Moses saw Israel as a special people set apart from all the world. Not what they did but who they were lingered in his thoughts. "O Israel," he observed, "who is like you, a people saved by the Lord?" No one was like Israel. Israel was a nation singled out by God and set apart for Him. With Israel, Moses had wandered for forty homeless years seeking refuge in the wilderness. He longed that they, like he, would find their sufficiency in the great God who had gone before them searching out a place for them to pitch their tents. To those people his final words of encouragement were, "The eternal God is thy refuge, and underneath are the everlasting arms."

On the very day that Moses' task of preparation was completed, he climbed to the top of Mount Pisgah. The time for parting had come. Entrance to the land was imminent. With the conclusion of his work came the conclusion of his life. It had been a long life, spent in triads of forty years each. In the first, he was a prince. In the second, he was a shepherd. In the third, he was a friend of God. In the palace he had luxury. In Midian he had security. In the wilderness he had neither. But there he walked and talked with God. Now it was time for his last dialogue with the Lord. It was brief and to the point.

"This is the land that I promised to Abraham, to Isaac, and to Jacob. I promised it to their descendants, and I have caused you to see it. But you will not go over."

There was no reason for Moses to die. He was neither feeble nor disabled. His eyesight was strong. His natural strength had not decreased. But it had been decided that he would die here, and the final dialogue was a mere formality. Moses was content to look at the land and to know that even before the dialogues ended at Mount Pisgah, God had already had the last word.

Study Guide

HOW DOES A BELIEVER AVOID BITTERNESS?

SCRIPTURE: Numbers 20, 27; Deuteronomy 1:37; 3:23-26; 33, 34

DOES BECOMING A BELIEVER GUARANTEE THAT ONE WILL NEVER FACE AN UNFAIR SITUATION? No, of course it doesn't. Think for a moment about unfair situations in which you or an acquaintance has been involved. Many such situations lead to bitterness in the heart of believers, sometimes subconscious, sometimes open and active. From a human standpoint, the incident at Meribah might appear to be an unfair situation. Let's discover why.

Scripture Exercise, Part 1

Who was more worthy to enter the land, Moses or the Israelites?

1. How did Israel feel about the land (Numbers 14:31)? _____
   _____ How did Moses feel about the land (Deuteronomy 3:23-25)? _____
   _____

2. On the basis of what you have learned in this course, how would you describe Israel's feelings for Moses? _____
   _____

   On many occasions Israel was spared judgment because Moses
   p _ _ _ _ _ for them. He saw Israel as a people unlike any other,
   a people s _ _ _ _ by _ _ _ _ _ _ _ (Deuteronomy 33:29).

3. On the basis of what you have learned in this course, how

91

would you describe Israel's attitude toward God's leading in the wilderness? _____

How is God's leading through the wilderness described by Moses (Deuteronomy 1:31, 33)? _____

_____

4. On the basis of what you have learned in this course, contrast Israel's and Moses' sensitivity (or lack of it) toward God's dealing with disobedience. _____

Do you think that Moses knew the disobedient are always dispensable? _____ Why or why not? _____

From the foregoing exercise it should be evident that if anyone entered the land because of love for the land, love for the Lord, or "worthiness," it should have been Moses. But that is human reasoning. God was not concerned with worthiness. Question 5 will focus on that with which He was concerned.

5. God brought the people of Israel to the land because (a) He knew future generations would appreciate it. (b) The generation that had grown up in the wilderness had earned the right to it. (c) Their ancestors had earned the right to it. (d) God had promised it to Abraham, Isaac, and Jacob.

God did not allow Moses to go into the land because (a) He was less deserving than the Israelites. (b) He disobeyed God, and that was the punishment for disobedience. (c) He had an Ethiopian wife.

Scripture Exercise, Part 2
How did Moses react to his punishment?
1. After Moses was told he could not enter the land, what was his first concern (Numbers 27:15-17)? _____

_____

Part of Moses' task now became that of preparing _____ to lead the Israelites to the land (Numbers 27:18-23).

2. The book of Deuteronomy contains the words that Moses spoke to Israel as they were about to enter the land. Why did he give this address (Deuteronomy 1:1-3)? _____
_____

3. How did Moses *feel* about not entering the land (Deuteronomy 3:23-25)? _____
_____

4. Why did Moses drop the subject after that conversation (Deuteronomy 3:26)? _____
_____

5. Did personal disappointment cause Moses to forsake his task (Deuteronomy 3:28)? _____

6. What was the state of Moses' health when he died (Deuteronomy 34:7)? _____
_____

SUMMARIZE: Moses clearly demonstrated a mature faith as he took the consequences of his sin and went on with his task. He avoided bitterness by submitting himself to the will of God even when it was unpleasant to him. To avoid bitterness, a believer must measure himself against God's yardstick and never against some other believer.

HOW DID MOSES' FAITH GROW?
From *commitment* to *reluctant obedience* to *implicit trust* to an *unswerving belief in the promises of God* to *submission to the will of God.*